The Victo
Daughter

The Victory Daughter

a memoir

Laura Scott
Elissa Cottle

First published in 2019 by
4 Square Books, an imprint of Ebooks LLC

Type set in Minion Pro and Optima

ISBN 978-1-61766-283-6

Publishing enquiries: maenadest@protonmail.com

Dedicated to my daughter, Ainsley.
May you always find the best in every situation.
Stand firm, keep your faith strong.

CHAPTER 1

Ocean Deep

I begin the birth rumble far too early. It's only 27 weeks into the 38-week journey my parents are wishing for, conception to healthy baby. The first two children in my family of origin perish at their births. My mother and father cling to hope that I will come to them alive. But they brace themselves for another childbirth tragedy.

My mother has developed preeclampsia during the pregnancy, which threatens her liver and heart. The doctors tell my parents that my impending premature birth is dangerous to both mother and child, and that they may face the choice of which of us would die, in order for the other to be saved. It is an awful, but immediate decision.

Before they wheel my mother into the operating room to split her open in a long vertical emergency C-section, my parents say their goodbyes to each other and instruct the doctors to save me, if it comes down to that.

In utero the force of me almost kills my mother. I am torn from her body nearly three months too soon. We both emerge from the birthing battlefield of Loyola Medical Center in Chicago still breathing. I am hooked up to an incubator, given a 20 percent chance of survival. My mother's chances are no better. After the birth, my mother's body fills up with fluid, and she temporarily goes blind. In the first three days, her doctors give no assurances that she will live.

My father is the only member of the family on his feet, going back and forth between the near-death beds of wife and daughter. As if a desperate token of love, my dad gives me his wedding ring. My little arm fits entirely through the ring, up to my elbow. Mom is hospitalized for a month after my birth; I manage to make it out of there in three months.

In the years that follow, there are periods when my mother is well. Then her end of the teeter-totter dips again. Suddenly the playground where she loves being a mother turns into a war zone where she fights for her lungs, liver, bones and blood.

Her sickness is a rogue member of our household that keeps my father and I on call to administer damage control. Every winter pneumonia kidnaps my mother and holds her hostage in the hospital.

Loyalty to my mother runs deep. Yet sometimes I am engulfed, gripping a life raft with my fingernails, hoping to save her from what lurks in her body. My love for her is an ocean, but I am drowning in it, knowing I can't do for her what she did for me—save my life.

CHAPTER 2

One Line

I am tiny but determined. I arrive with body parts intact. Among the babies born in the U.S. in 1984, I'm the first to survive healthy after starting only at 1 pound, 12 ounces.

The March of Dimes helps me beat the odds for babies my size. Since the 1950s, the nonprofit organization has championed medical care to bring fragile babies to life and well-being, and to prevent premature births.

At age 6, I return the favor to the March of Dimes by accepting the job as their 1991 ambassador. The post includes a year-long tour of 19 national and international appearances, capturing the eyes of the world with my story of survival, showing no outward signs of struggle.

We are flown first class to New York City from our home in Naperville, Illinois, a suburb of Chicago. It's a cold, windy New Year's Day in 1991 as my family of three gets ready to greet America from a stage watched by millions. I put on my fancy red coat, looking sweet next to my mother, so pretty in her long fur. Dad wears covers over his nice shoes to protect them from the snow; whenever I see the shoe covers I know we are going somewhere special.

We climb into a limo. I love riding in this shiny car because inside I get anything I want to drink, plus there's candy in the deal.

As soon as we reach the studio of "Good Morning America," I am rushed into hair and makeup. After all the fuss over my face, I am topped off with a ton of hair spray, and then "miked."

Before I reach the on-air set, our press manager rushes toward me holding some kind of blue wrap that I don't know what to do with. Our traveling photographer helps me into it. "Put your arms up," he instructs, and pulls the blue sash into position over my shoulder and down to my hip.

"Momma, what does this say?" In huge letters the sash declares my new identity: "March of Dimes National Ambassador."

"You are to wear this whenever we go someplace; it's special," my mother explains.

She is in her own dressing room, getting her hair and makeup done as she sips on a cup of water and clears her throat. She is preparing to speak for the first time as mother of the ambassador. She looks very serious, and it makes me nervous. I am on edge because she is on edge.

Finally it's time to step in front of the cameras. I hop up onto the big suede couch on the stage, with the microphone hooked to my sash, and sit down in the middle, my parents on either side of me. I am beaming, thrilled to be between them as they both gaze upon me, their living, healthy daughter.

We get the signal that we are on the air. Co-anchors Joan Lunden and Charlie Gibson introduce us, and ask how the March of Dimes has made a difference in our lives. Mom speaks first. She tells how the March of Dimes helped her before, during, and after her pregnancy with me, including all the medicines I am given to keep me alive. Then the question turns to me.

"Laura, why should we help the March of Dimes?"

I remember my one line: "To help babies like me."

But, to my mother's horror, as I'm speaking the sound is garbled for the audience because I've been absently fiddling with my sash and dislodge the microphone.

I look at my mom. She is glaring at me.

CHAPTER 3

The Victory Daughter

"Ten years ago, I felt as if I had lost my future," says my mother, in one of her many rallying speeches for the March of Dimes.

Candyce Krumwiede draws in her audience by taking them behind the curtain of her personal life.

"I was a woman who had just buried her second baby. I had no direction in life. I had no self-esteem. I felt very inadequate as a woman," she confesses.

"But one hope remained—to become a mother."

She goes on to tell my birth story. The story that mothers retell over and over throughout their lives, never quite getting over their amazement at the feat of creating an entire human being.

But even though she has created a human being, she's terrified that I may not survive because I am so tiny.

". . . and if she did survive, she could have multiple problems—bleeds of the brain, heart and lung damage, problems seeing and hearing," she says.

"I remember, when Laura was in the isolette, she used to work and flex her minuscule toes and feet. I would sit and stroke her transparent skin, and her toothpick-sized legs and arms, and daydream that someday she would be a normal healthy child.

"It was that hope that sutured me on as I watched the machines breathing for her, and all the beepers were going off. The nurses were pricking her hands and feet hourly for blood tests."

The setting for her speech this time was a March of Dimes event in Virginia for families, which included fun activities for kids, including a magic performance.

My mother recounts that when she had me, she almost felt like a magician herself, "pulling this little baby out of a hat who began to beat the odds of infant mortality and to flourish medically and physically."

The credit for this amazing feat goes to the March of Dimes, my mother tells her audience of potential donors.

"Thank goodness for the March of Dimes," she says.

"For over 50 years the March of Dimes has created an awareness, and a body of volunteers, to ensure that a mother's pre- and post-natal care is important. The March of Dimes has been delivering small miracles for many years. The first was conquering polio. After that, the March of Dimes did not sit on its laurels. It turned its stride to the more complex problem of birth defects, low birth weight and infant mortality.

"I have lived the failures as well as the successes of the March of Dimes mission," concludes Mom.

Then, like a warrior woman, she marches up to the pinnacle of the mountain of dimes, and plants her flag, which shall ever pull and ripple throughout my life.

"I have my victory in Laura."

CHAPTER 4

Trying To Be Good

I am a dabbling young musician. One day it's a brass baritone horn. Another day it's a cello.

My house is behind the playground of my school. But to go home, I am never allowed to cut through the schoolyard grass to my own back yard. Everyone has to walk on the sidewalk. This is unfair. As I lug my huge instrument, it's a long way home on the sidewalk going all the way around the school. My tiny curls bounce frantically, and I'm drenched in sweat by the time I get home, the stiff vinyl handle of my black cello case digging into my palm.

"What are you carrying now, Laura?" my mother asks, with only a hint of sarcasm.

There's the side of me that always wants to be good. That I owe it to my mother to hold up her Laura flag and be this bottomless vessel of living goodness, reimbursing her for putting her life at risk so I could be born. She never says anything of the sort. Nonetheless, my irrational sense of debt to her rattles in the back of my head, especially when my mother talks about how to live one's best.

"Bloom where you are planted" is one of her favorite inspirational phrases. Yes, show your loveliest self even when your garden is wilted—it's a noble sentiment. But when trying to be good feels maddening, a streak of mayhem rears up in the ground beneath my pretty flowers.

There are days when school rules can go to hell. I sneak through the schoolyard like a thief who raided the orchestra vault. Sometimes I make it to my yard unnoticed by the authorities. Sometimes I am nabbed by a teacher who has no compassion for helpless, musically gifted children—they should find a job in a meat-packing plant where the subjects can't break any rules.

My mom enjoys watching me and my friends playing at recess, our laughter musically drifting into her afternoon. I see her working in the garden.

"Hi, Mom!" I yell across the playground, outside for gym class.

My gym teacher, a schoolyard Gestapo, scolds me for interrupting the class.

By contrast, Mom often greets me with a plate of fresh cookies when I come home, talking under my breath about the oppressive conditions of elementary school. She hugs me tight when I'm in the door. I guess the day isn't that bad.

Making it through young girlhood without too many missteps, I am rewarded on my 13th birthday with a surprise from Mom.

"Laura, you're a young lady now. Let's get your ears pierced!"

I am thrilled. On a cold October day in Chicago, we scope out all the cosmetic stores to find the best price for one's ears to be pierced. Merle Norman Cosmetic Studio. Walking into the store laden with all kinds of beauty accessories, I feel conspicuous going past the long aisle crowded by mannequin heads wearing wigs. Among the blank faces of blondes and brunettes are lots of shiny earrings on display. My ear lobes perk up. In the back of the store is a tall chair that swivels.

"Sit down here," says the Merle Norman official,

who looks like she's had a very long career as a piercing professional. Her heavy, gold-colored earrings dangle almost to her shoulders.

"First I have to clean your ears," she says, plucking cotton balls out of a jar with expertise.

"Will it hurt?" I ask my mom.

"Just sit still, Laura. The more you fret, the more it will hurt."

I clench my jaw. I'll get through this and then I can wear real earrings like a grown-up woman.

My ears burn and sting from the punctures. But I get to pick out tiny diamonds for my first pair of earrings.

"Make sure you wash and dry your ears around the diamonds every single night. And keep the earrings in for six weeks until your ears heal," says the piercer. "But after you can take them out, never sleep in earrings."

My mom gives me a look to emphasize the lady's instructions. But can I be good? A few years later, after my ears have graduated from their first little diamonds, my parents generously buy me a larger pair of diamond studs. And I sleep in them. The holes in my ears stretch and eventually rip open my earlobes. I am full of shame when I tell my mom what happened.

"They are ruined now, Laura. I'm glad that we paid money to have holes ripped into your ears," she said, slamming my bedroom door.

A week later she said I'd have to get my ears sewn up. I hear her tell the dermatologist on the phone that I need my ears repaired because I didn't follow directions. I am so mad at myself.

After the surgical earlobe procedure, the dermatologist says I'll have to wait six weeks before I can get my ears pierced again. I look at Mom.

"You have got to be kidding me," she says.

Once we get into the car, I ask her if I can please get them re-pierced.

"No. You can't take care of them. If you do, I'm not paying for it."

I save my allowance every Sunday for months until I have enough. Not happy, my mom drives me back to Merle Norman's. The same lady is there, planted behind the piercing chair like she never moved.

"I will listen this time," I tell her. She rolls her eyes and looks at my mother.

The ears stay intact until I get to college. Then I find myself twisting my earrings all the time to deal with anxiety. The ears start to rip again. I am too ashamed to tell my mom this time. I try wearing big earrings to cover up the overstretched holes in my earlobes. Eventually the holes heal by themselves, almost. But now when I try to wear earrings, it's too painful to keep them in very long.

CHAPTER 5

Man in the White Hat

You could say my mother and I both find our men out of the same sticky Hallmark TV special. My mother first spots my dad on campus at Purdue University and knows he would be the one. Fast forward some 25 years, when I am in the back row of a steep, 900-seat sociology class at Purdue and spy the man I would marry. He is sitting down in the front, long blonde curls poking out of his white Wyoming Cowboys baseball hat, and I know.

"There's a cute boy in my class," I text my mom. (The Hallmark violins begin to swell.)

He and his friends are doing a crossword puzzle, laughing. I don't try to make my way through the masses to put myself in his path today. But I try to figure out how I can as soon as possible.

A couple of days later I'm sitting in my sociology study group when the teacher says, "Emerson, would you come up and move something for me?"

Who's Emerson? I turn around. Bingo.

A week later I bump into him at a party at his fraternity house. In my mind, our relationship has advanced significantly since I spotted him in class, so naturally I run up to him and give him a hug.

"You're here. I knew I'd find you!"

He recognizes me, and looks like a man in an ambush. Plus, he's with another girl, and I quickly back away. But am not deterred in the least.

I tell a friend of mine at Purdue about him. She immediately appoints herself an ally in my pursuit of the man I would commit to for life. Soon thereafter, at another party, my friend is writing my phone number on a scrap of paper and handing it to him like a proxy serving him a warrant for love.

"Laura really likes you—you should call her!"

A week later he calls, when I'm at my grandparents' house. He leaves a message out of a fairy tale.

"Hey, your friend told me to call you, so that's what I'm doing."

When I call him back, we talk for two hours. That leads to a date for coffee. My next move is to snag him for my sorority's formal winter dance, just three weeks away. Surrounded by my Pi Beta Phi sisters for moral support, I text him.

"Do you have a suit at school?"

"Yeah, why?"

"Because you're going to need it to go to the winter formal with me."

Within minutes, the reply sweeps into my phone like open arms in a field of Hallmark daisies.

"Yeah, I'll go."

He's a freshman, but I'm a whole year ahead in the game, planning our decades together. At the formal in my long, purple dress I dance with him, my head on his shoulder like a pillow in the house of a long-married couple.

On our walk home, he puts his coat around my chilly shoulders. This becomes one of his signature gestures. Whenever I'm cold, he's pulling off his jacket, or his shirt, his lovely shoulders bare in his undershirt, offering me a warm layer out of a poem.

After the formal, Emerson becomes a fixture at the sorority house. He loves being surrounded by 70 girls, but he only offers his coat to me.

CHAPTER 6

Puppies and Broccoli

I am in a puffy pink dress and pink bow. My mother is curling my hair—until she drops the curling iron on my shoulder.

"Ouch, Mom!"

"I'm sorry, Laura. I'm nervous."

I look in the mirror and see her anxious face behind me as she is glossing my hair with hairspray, her strained mouth painted in bright lipstick. Why she is so nervous? We are just going to meet one more grown-up along the trail of so many who want to meet me. Little Ambassador Laura Krumwiede.

President George Herbert Walker Bush opens the door to the Oval Office and welcomes us in. Security guards and the press surround us. I am underwhelmed.

I don't like how it smells in here, like moth balls. And the lights are turned up so bright. I skip past the president, my blonde shiny curls bouncing up and down, and then let out a scream—puppies!

Puppies at the White House? Millie, President Bush's English Springer Spaniel, recently has given birth to six cute black and white spotted puppies. Finally this ambassador thing has gone beyond boring speeches, around a bunch of grown-ups getting overly excited just because I can walk and talk like any other kid. Puppies are something to get excited about!

It's my mother's 35th birthday, Jan. 24, 1991, and we are spending it with Millie's puppies and a president. Mr. Bush is sitting in a big comfy chair. His desk is huge and stacked with papers. I spend my time under that desk, with the puppies, letting my adult surrogates, David and Candyce Krumwiede, do the talking.

I finally climb out from under the desk and look up into the tall man's face. I have thought of a good question to ask.

"Do you have to eat broccoli?"

The president sighs.

"Yes, I eat broccoli, so you have to as well," says the commander in chief.

That seals it for my mom's dinner table rules. I look at her and know that I can never complain about eating broccoli again. The president has issued an order to the ambassador for the March of Dimes, and she would hold that over me for the rest of her life.

CHAPTER 7

A Promise

I can't shake the weighted notion that after putting my parents through hell as a baby, it's my responsibility to forever stay healthy for them. I never relinquish the image of my mother nearly dying to bring me into the world. My parents endure a lifetime of worry in my first months clinging to life. Going forward, it's the least I can do to keep my body in one piece.

I maintain that unspoken promise, more or less, through childhood and early adulthood. At age 23, my body makes other plans.

At college, I represent the fourth generation in my family graduating from Purdue University, in West Lafayette, Indiana. I am getting my degree in early childhood education, and doing an internship at an Early Head Start child care center with infants. In the week before Thanksgiving, I bend over to pick up a child, and a sharp pain stabs me in the left side.

I take some deep breaths. Maybe I'm coming down with a chest cold. But my inhale produces another frightening pain in the upper part of my chest. I am not going to get sick. Especially now, so close to graduation in December. I let it go for the day.

A sharp pain in my left side wakes me up in the middle of the night, in a sweat. I take myself to the campus health clinic. The nurse asks me where it hurts, and quickly diagnoses me with bronchitis.

"But I haven't been coughing," I tell her, skeptical.

"Well, you must be for the pain you're having."

She gives me an inhaler and tells me to take three Advils every other hour. I go home to bed and sleep hard and long. I am going to kick this. My parents will be in town this weekend for Homecoming. The next day, I get up, get dressed and go to back to work.

On my way there I think I'm going to throw up. I never get sick to my stomach. I turn around, rush home and throw up. Defeated, I call work and tell them I won't be in that day. I go to bed at 9 a.m. and don't wake up until

5 in the afternoon when my friends call wanting to go out. All I want to do is go back to sleep. I'm still in pain and the Advil is not helping.

I take myself back to the clinic. It's late at night and lonely, waiting for the doctor to come in. Finally he arrives and tells me to follow him to get an X-ray. It's a long walk, in the basement of the building, in and out of hallways. At last we get to the X-ray lab. I undress in a small dark bathroom. A nurse takes the X-ray. I peek at the screen and see a gray mass on the left side of my chest.

"What is *that*?"

"It's just one of your organs," she says, nonchalant.

I get dressed, uneasy, and walk back to the front desk.

"We'll call you when we have the results. Keep taking Advil," says the helpful nurse.

I drive to Emerson's house, sobbing. Something is wrong. The nurses are not listening to me. I have little energy to fight. Later I go back to my place and sleep for three straight days. Emerson stays with me on an air mattress in the living room. Because I'm in so much pain, I don't want him to sleep beside me and accidentally roll over and hit my side.

The X-ray comes back clear. But I'm in bad shape. Emerson feeds me, and brings me Advil and water. Eventually he has to turn his attention back to studying. I use the inhaler for my alleged "cough," sucking in the distasteful air through the plastic mouth piece. It makes me nauseous. I am sweaty and shaky. I call my mom.

"Can you come? Now? Something is wrong."

Since I already have plans to go home to Chicago the next week, the campus doctor says I might as well see my family doctor there, "to see what is going on." Good idea, Doc.

Back in Chicago, I have plans for a week-long training to become certified in infant massage. It's very important to me. I want to heighten my professional skills to include the healing care of massage. I will always have the drive to support children up close. The image of myself as a tiny, frightened infant never leaves me. I can't remember being that infant. But in my colorful imagination, I never stop watching that newborn in a sterile incubator alone, needing human touch.

I do not want this infiltrator in my chest to mess up my carefully laid plans! At home for Thanksgiving break,

I get another chest X-ray and an exam, and I'm told I'll get results in a couple of days. But I'm not going to wait home and fret. The following Monday, I attend the first eight-hour session of the infant massage training.

I return to the training on Tuesday, and make it through the day, but get sick to my stomach with a terrible migraine. I dismiss it. I am just worn out from the intensive training. Wednesday when I get home from training, my mom tells me the doctor called and they saw something on my left kidney. But not to worry—it's probably a cyst.

Usually I rush to the Internet to look up any health concern. This time I am not going to do that. I will be fine. The so-called cyst doesn't break my exciting momentum toward becoming a certified infant massage therapist. On Thursday we get another call. It is not a cyst. I need to get looked at by a urologist. I ask the doctor if I can wait a month, until after graduation in December. The answer is no.

I finish the massage training on Friday. The next week, my mother and I go to the urologist. She and I are glued at the hip, but I am a grown woman now and she stays in the waiting room. I nervously hand the doctor the disc of my

X-ray. He leaves the room for what seems like a long time. When he finally returns, he comes in and shuts the door.

"Yep, you have cancer," he says, matter of fact.

"What do you mean? How? What do I have to do?"

He says it's renal cell carcinoma and I have to have my left kidney removed immediately. He directs me to speak to the receptionist to schedule the surgery.

"So once I have surgery, then it will be gone."

"Let's hope that's all you have to do," he says. Not helpful.

I'm numb but defiant. I don't believe him. I want a second opinion. I drag myself back out to the waiting room. I see my mother sitting there, and don't want to give her this news. I don't want her to accept this unreliable diagnosis and fall apart. I don't want to disappoint her.

"It's cancer," I tell her, guilty that I let this killer into my body. She put her life on the line for me to be healthy. She doesn't deserve this. She breaks down, falling to the floor. Then gets up and gets angry. She is my mother.

"I need to talk to that doctor," she said, mad.

"Don't believe him," I said, joining forces with her. "We are getting a second opinion."

I don't want anyone to know because it isn't true. I don't have cancer. And right away my mom calls my dad and Emerson. Then she finds the best urologist at Loyola Medical Center. That place saved me once. Listen up, people. I'm back.

We get an appointment for the following week. Waiting for the appointment is awful. I'm 23. I'm too young to need two Vicodin to get through pain.

For this appointment I want my parents in the room. I am unsteady and feel unable to retain information. The nurse is told our family does not have a history of cancer.

"This is a little strange that you are being tested for renal cell cancer because it usually affects 65-year-old male smokers," says the nurse. "You are a healthy 23-year-old girl."

That makes me feel a little better. Maybe they got it wrong. Maybe I don't have it. Then the doctor comes in the room, after reviewing my scan.

"Yes, this is renal cell carcinoma," pronounces Dr. Second Opinion.

My stomach drops. The guilt sets in again. There is pain in my parents' eyes. I let them down. I don't want their only daughter to have cancer. I look back on the last three months: the nausea, vomiting, hair loss. I have dropped 20 pounds. I have night sweats. I tried to tell myself it is all stress related.

Like the last doctor, this one said I need immediate surgery to remove my entire left kidney. And he is a little concerned that he might have to remove my ureter if the cancer has spread that far. If that is the case, there is a greater chance I would need chemo. That sounds scarier than the surgery.

I am losing weight by the day, becoming scary thin. I'm extremely tired and need constant pain killers. I sleep with my mom, holding her hand. The surgery is scheduled for two days after Christmas.

Before that is graduation. I don't have the strength to go, but I badly want to be there. The day of, I take two pain pills and put on my cap and gown. It's strange seeing my friends at this exciting occasion in our lives, knowing I have cancer hiding under my black gown. I imagine people are whispering about me, but I know everyone is really rooting for me.

I ignore the pain and hold up my head, walk across

the stage, and shake my professor's hand. *I am not a cancer patient, I am a Purdue graduate.* I am thrilled to get my degree. I have worked hard for it. I got past learning challenges, and I was dedicated. I got this thing! I'm proud to hug my parents, telling them "I did it!"

Then we go home and wait for surgery day. Everyone keeps telling me to be strong and that I can beat this! I appreciate their support, but I'm also a bit annoyed. *I don't need them to tell me I'll beat this. I know I will. There is no other option.*

On the eve of my surgery, it's a party at my house. A cheerleading squad just for me—all my relatives and close friends, from college and childhood, are there. People play games, watch Purdue football on TV, and laugh. It's nice to have people there to distract me and show their support.

However, I want to feel my feelings, to think about what is about to happen. I am about to lose a kidney. I sneak away to my room. *What are they all laughing and so happy about? Don't they know what tomorrow is?* Sitting on my bed, I pray.

Make it be OK, whatever happens.

After my private consult upstairs, I go back down and enjoy my family and friends. I have to be at the hospital at 4 a.m. the next morning. But when Emerson tucks me in bed, says he loves me, and turns out the lights, I start to cry. *What if I don't make it through tomorrow?* Emerson comes back to bed and cries with me.

"You're strong, you can do this," says the knight of all boyfriends. This time I am glad to hear the encouragement.

The next day at the hospital, I am prepped and put into a gown. My minister is there and we say a prayer over my bed. My family is by my side. *I'm fine. I will get out of here in one piece.* Then the doctor comes in.

"Give your mom your glasses and a kiss goodbye," he said.

Simple instructions I am not prepared for. I come undone. Don't want to leave her. I want the strength she gave me 23 years ago at my birth in this hospital. When they wheel me away I am sobbing and scared. I look back at my family, all in tears. I remind myself I am lucky to have them. I don't say goodbye.

"I'll see you in seven hours," I tell them.

In the room alone waiting for my anesthesia, I gather

my strength, pray to God, and finally reach a sense of peace. This doctor is the best. He'll get all the cancer. I wake up seven hours later to my family standing by my side.

"They got it all! You are cancer free!" they are saying. It is a full-organ, church choir song.

"Are you sure?" I'm not so sure.

I'm in a lot of pain. Bloated from the gas they used to blow up my stomach. I'm exhausted and sleep all day.

In my stay in the hospital over several days, I do not want to be labeled a cancer survivor or cancer patient. I don't have cancer anymore. Then I try to get out of bed and walk down the hall. I can't move, feeling permanently bent over. But I have to push through it. Emerson walks me up and down the hallways at 1 mph. I am determined. I don't not want people to feel sad for me.

Sent home to rest for three months, I don't protest; it's still difficult to move. My bed sounds good. I'll have a lot of time to think. What will life be like, post cancer? I still don't like the sound of "survivor." I turn to my Bible, with its purple cover, on the bedside table. The book sits next to a yellow marker, which is still how I practice my time with the Bible, highlighting the particularly inspiring passages with the color of a bright sun.

And we know that all things work together for good to them that love God, to them who are the called according to his purpose.—Romans 8:28

In my new-found job—recovery—the good news is, at 23, the body heals well. I want to go back to work as soon as possible. I want to be with my preschool kids. I am their teacher. I want to continue making a difference in their lives. In May, five months after the surgery, I go back to work, glad to have the children to think about instead of myself. On the outside, I look normal.

But my body isn't all in. On the inside, the healing process needs more time. I go back home, and don't return to the preschool until September, finally ready for duty. Refusing to answer death's knock, for the second time, gives me a stronger sense of myself and a deeper relationship with God. Emerson and I get engaged the following May.

In the middle of a rainstorm, dance. The water feels good on my face.

CHAPTER 8

Back to Day One

A few weeks after our day in the White House, we are whisked to our next official visit on behalf of the March of Dimes at Loyola Medical Center, where I was born smaller than a puppy. As usual, the room is crowded with people. My mother grips my hand tight.

"Stay with me," she says in a firm voice.

I had made my first spectacular appearance into the world here, the day I was born. But today, back in the same place, I can't see how I am going to beat *that* act of God.

In here, life is a hold-your-breath nonstop loop of birthing, dying, suffering and healing. Once again I am the one getting top billing on this life-or-death stage, armored in the blue banner of victory I wear across my small frame. Princess of hope.

I exhale when I spot my grandmother, aunt, uncle and all of my cousins. They are sitting in front of a table set with 10 microphones, and a podium. There are huge cameras and people with tape recorders directly behind them. I start to rush to my cousins, but my mother jerks me back.

"This is not the time to play! We have to give an interview."

Obediently I follow my mother and father to the podium for a press conference. The interview airs on CBS, NBC, FOX television, WGN-TV in Chicago, and WBBM radio. I sit next to my mother, my father next to her. I can barely see over the microphones, and the faces of the huge crowd disappear in the bright camera lights. Then someone grabs my hand. I turn to the right and it's my grandma. Her bright eyes and huge smile immediately calm me down.

I listen to my parents repeat our newsworthy story, starting with my mother's pregnancy, her journey to meet me, facing many medical complications along the way, each requiring frightening decisions, emerging triumphant with the life-saving support of the March of Dimes. Then I hear my cue.

"Laura, why should we give money to help the March of Dimes?"

Still blinking in the lights, I don't know who asked me, but I remember my mother's explicit directions before we got here, hovering above me like the Wizard of Oz in his powerful voice:

Look into the camera and say, "To help babies like me."

My mother is brilliant—the line works like magic. Huge applause bursts into the air, a chaos of clapping and crying. Still holding my grandmother's hand I look at her; she is smiling and crying.

I am a celebrity, but first I am a little girl, not able to grasp the breadth of my influence. How did I make all these people cry?

CHAPTER 9

Real Violins

We date through college, through my bout of cancer without a flinch from Emerson. We are the first of our friends to be married. The support of our family and friends at our wedding is especially tangible after growing closer during cancer's dark tunnel through my body.

After college Emerson moves to Denver and gets a job in construction, while I stay back in Illinois with my parents, planning our big day.

On Oct. 10, 2009, we have a church wedding at Grace United Methodist, our family's place of worship in Naperville, with 120 guests. My bridesmaid party of six, in flowing purple fabric, includes my best friend Kathryn as my matron of honor, Emerson's sister Nicole, and four cousins who feel like sisters, Erin, Rachel, Sara and Colleen.

All standing in traditional, sharp black, Emerson's six groomsmen include his cousin Eli as best man, friends from childhood Jimmy, Jake, Tom and Levi, and my best guy friend Kyle from college.

There are violinists and cellists. Emerson meets me at the altar in a black tux and maroon tie. He manages to keep the coat with tails on through the wedding vows.

He is so out of that coat by the time we get to Napa for our honeymoon in the wine country of California.

CHAPTER 10

Giant Bulls

There are cameras and tall, tall men following me through a tunnel, from the locker room to the basketball court of the Chicago Bulls. My dad is walking with me.

"What are we doing?" I ask.

I only remember my father responding with a huge smile plastered on his face.

When we arrive onto the court, I feel like I have suddenly shrunk to the size of an ant. The giants around me are practicing their shots before the game, and if I don't watch it, I'm afraid any one of them could step on me and I'd be squashed. Suddenly someone pulls me in front of a gaggle of cameras.

"Look here! Look here!" shout the photographers.

My face is hot and my eyes can't focus, as cameras are clicking in the eager hands of photo journalists and bystanders. Then I look up and see three of the giants standing over me, one of them holding a basketball.

"Laura, this is Johnny Paxson," says my dad. Mom is beside him, smiling.

Standing at 6-feet-2, Johnny kindly bends down on one knee. "Do you know how to shoot a basketball?"

I shoot him a grin. "Yes!"

I take the ball in my small hands. The hoop is hanging even higher above my head than Johnny Paxon. With all my might I heave the ball up, but it just bounces way below the basket. All the nice giants give me a sympathetic smile.

Johnny feels confident that the Bulls will win the game that day (and they do). But to win the heart of the March of Dimes poster girl, he makes a quick pivot in strategy, offering me his knee to sit on.

"What's your favorite thing at school?"

It's pretty cool to be on the court with famous basketball players. But what I am really excited about is the soft pretzel and cotton candy I'll get once we are in the stands, watching the game.

(The pretzel and cotton candy are still my favorite things on a game day.)

CHAPTER 11

Succinct Prayer

I am six months into my marriage and we launch into a family—with an 8-week-old puppy. We are in Littleton, Colorado, a Denver suburb, living in an apartment. But George, our own English Springer Spaniel (move over, Millie), makes a strong case for buying our first house.

On moving day, as I am unloading boxes, it occurs to me that I have missed a period. But I put the thought aside. I'm excited to make a home in our new house, a tan split-level, three-bedroom with a big back yard in Littleton.

I'm 25 years old, working with young children in my church's preschool and in love with my husband. After fighting to survive as a baby, then spinning around like a caped Batgirl to slay cancer as a young woman, I have righted my path to health, world. Don't mess with me. I have a strong will, plus I've got Emerson and George in my corner now, who will growl if need be.

Sitting in the bathroom, the puppy at my feet, the test stick is in my hand. It's positive.

"George, I'm pregnant!"

George wiggles and kisses my face. Then I start to shake. Is it true? Is it real? I immediately call Emerson.

"Don't freak out till we know for sure," says my husband, typically calm. But he allows a glimmer of excitement in his voice.

Please, God, let this be true! Succinct.

The next day I'm at the doctor's office for a blood test. Since my tenure as a March of Dimes big shot, looking at babies in their incubators, I have always wanted to have my own baby one day. I want to change my family's story about babies who are frail and don't always make it.

"Yes, you're pregnant," says the doctor, closing the door.

My future baby is six weeks along. The doctor tells me to see my OB-GYN next week.

Important doctor's appointments are often a family affair with my parents. While my mom and dad are thrilled by the news, they are in their new home in South Carolina and don't hop on a plane to Colorado for this momentous but routine appointment with the OB. Emerson can't get away from work. I ask a girlfriend to meet me there. Doctors make me anxious.

We are in the dark ultrasound room. I'm lying on the padded table as the tech is gliding the cold, gel-covered wand across my belly. It's silent; no one is speaking except the buzz of the machine, framing the picture of my future. The screen looks like a bunch of lines and gray mass.

"Where's the baby?" My heart is in my throat.

The tech says she is not allowed to confirm or deny anything. "Um, let me get the doctor quick. I'll be right back."

I know what the doctor will say.

"I'm sorry, Laura, there is no heartbeat."

I'm not shocked. But still crushed. I look at my friend and she knows I need space. She hugs me and tells me to call her if I need anything. I feel like I have to gulp the air in that vacant room, my lungs squeezed when the doctor pronounced, in so many words, the time of death of someone I loved, sight unseen. The loneliness is deafening. I run to my car, fall into the seat like dead weight. I call my mom.

"I lost the baby," comes out in a muffled cry.

"Oh, baby," says Mom. "I'm sorry."

I know the sadness in her voice. Before losing her first two babies at birth, she had lost her first pregnancy to a miscarriage. We both feel my first pregnancy dropping like a stone into the abyss that carried away my tiny brother and sister, before we ever knew them.

"I have to have a D&C and have the baby taken out."

The name of the procedure is graphic—dilation and curettage. The cervix is dilated so the fetal tissue can be scraped away by the spoon-shaped curette. But I wanted to tell my mom out loud what is going to happen, like a bloody scream I had to let out. The doctor will be ripping something out of my body I so much want to keep.

I'm not ready for this appointment. Before going back to the doctor's office to face the D&C, I take a brief trip to Las Vegas to be with my friend Kathryn, my matron of honor, where she is living on a military base. We are both grieving. Just months after my wedding when she stood by my side, Kathryn lost her husband in Afghanistan. 1st

Lt. Joel Gentz was killed when his Medivac helicopter is shot down by the Taliban.

Several years later, I share the joy of Kathryn getting engaged.

CHAPTER 12

My Girlfriend Shirley

Can my place of honor in society, as ambassador for the March of Dimes, get even higher? You betcha. Like a girl playing Olympic jump rope, I jump up a notch when I am tapped by a Kentucky senator for the "the highest title of honor bestowed by the Commonwealth of Kentucky."

Senator Wendell Ford presents me with a certificate naming me a Kentucky Colonel on Aug. 30 of my sixth year, significantly widening my circle of associates. I am now in the ranks of, among other notables, two celebrities widely known in widely different ways—Kentucky Colonel Shirley Temple, the beloved child actress of the 1930s, and Kentucky Colonel Harland Sanders, founder of finger-lickin' Kentucky Fried Chicken.

Of course, the importance of these associations is lost on me at the time. But my mother is giddy at the thought of her little girl mentioned in the same breath with Shirley Temple, who she also adores.

Regardless of one's connections to Kentucky (I have none), commissions for Kentucky Colonels are given by the state to individuals from all places in recognition of noteworthy accomplishments and outstanding service to a community, state or the nation.

The title of Kentucky Colonel started in 1813 to recognize individuals of honor. Kentucky Colonels have grown into a large collection of charitable organizations, with chapters around the world. Some 85,000 have received this special recognition, bestowed upon well-known people and many others not publicly known. They are from all walks, chosen for their reputation of having high moral standards and a record of doing good works.

Like the other stops along my March of Dimes tour, I am not paying attention to meeting someone's high standards. At the top of my priorities is getting to swim at hotel pools.

"Can we go swimming?" I ask as soon as we get to the hotel in Lexington, Kentucky.

"Let's get settled first," says Mom, not excited about the pool.

My parents look at each other and give in.

We get into our room and quickly wriggle into our bathing suits. The pool at this hotel is tiny, but I don't care. It's water and I can turn into a mermaid (which sounds more doable than becoming a "colonel").

My mom sits at the side of the pool, dangling her feet in the water. My father rolls himself into a huge cannon ball, plunges in and splashes my mom. Even she is laughing. I beg my dad to throw me up in the air so I can land with a splash and soak Mom again.

She giggles. "Don't you dare, Laura Louise." I do anyway.

After a short while, suddenly Mom stands up. "We have a big day tomorrow and better get some sleep."

We slip and slosh our way back to our room. I'm so tired, I don't even change out of my bathing suit before falling asleep.

On the way to the ceremony, I am taken in by all the fields of horses out the window as we go by. Lots of white picket fences and hay bales. Growing up in Chicago, this scenery looks like something out a book or a TV show. *Do people really live around horses?*

Mom is standing at the podium with a microphone in her hand. Her hair is curled tight, and her green, flowery dress is bolstered by big, hidden shoulder pads. She's tall in her black high heels. I remember the heels vividly. She is so pretty in them, as they click clack along the floor, a sound every little girl loves to hear.

She is telling the crowd how the March of Dimes saved both of our lives, and would they please donate money for more research. She's wearing her serious face, so these people better listen up. It is the same face I see when I am in trouble. I know that *I* have no choice but to do as she says when that face appears.

There's lots of clapping as my father is pushing me up to the stage to stand next to my mom. Senator Ford is handing her the framed certificate. She then bends down to show it to me. It's in cursive which I can't read yet; all I see is my name in big bold letters.

I am envied by most of the Kentucky natives in that

room. Once again all I do is live my life and people are thanking me. It feels strange, like they are speaking a different language.

Years later, I find a letter my mom wrote me after my anointment as a Kentucky Colonel.

Laura, I am so proud of you and have fallen more in love with you all over again during this trip. You were such a trooper.

As an adult, I finally get what the fuss is about. And, by the way, my girlfriend Shirley became the first female Colonel in 1932. Just sayin'.

CHAPTER 13

Don't Go Having the Baby While I'm on the Mountain

Four months after the miscarriage I am pregnant again. This time Emerson comes with me to see the doctor. The baby has a very strong heartbeat.

But as I carry this pregnancy I'm always getting sick. I can't stand beef or chicken. When I'm not nauseous, I have cravings—I have to have bags of Cheetos and gallons of orange juice. I know it all means that I have a live baby in there pulling my gut strings, and I will endure whatever it takes to keep that baby growing.

It's a snowy day in Colorado. I'm 29 weeks along, relaxing on our soft, red couch, reading a magazine with a bag of Cheetos for company.

"Bye babe," says Emerson, chipper in his bright orange jacket and Denver Broncos visor hat. Gone are the long blonde curls that once beckoned me when I first spotted him at Purdue, then capped by the Wyoming Cowboys hat (from his parents' alma mater). His beautiful hair is cut short, but he still always has a hat on.

"I'm going skiing. Don't go having the baby while I'm on the mountain."

I roll my eyes at my hilarious husband. "Yeah, OK honey." No problem. I am glad to have peace and quiet in the house.

An hour after he after he leaves, the contractions kick in. Not terrible but crampy. By the time he gets home my contractions are five minutes apart and I feel awful.

Not yet, baby. I need you to hang in there longer.

"Don't take off your coat, we need to go to the hospital," I tell Emerson.

"You're kidding me, right?"

I am fighting to keep myself together in the car as our drive through the snow is slow torture, stuck behind a plow truck the whole way there. I can't be happier when we finally pull up to the ER.

"I'm 29 weeks and having contractions," I tell the hospital staff person.

She speeds me down the hall in a wheelchair. I get all hooked up to the machines, and the equipment shows us that the baby's heartbeat is strong. I breathe a sigh of relief. A moment of respite.

Then the contractions kick in again, this time a minute apart. The machines are beeping and flashing, like 911 loudspeakers coming from my thrashing uterus. My blood pressure spikes.

"You're going to stress the baby," the nurse warns me. "You need to be calm." Oh, sure. Easy.

The nurse turns off the lights and shuts the door to try to get me to relax. My body isn't getting the message. We soon find out that I have preeclampsia, the same dangerous pregnancy complication that almost killed my mother and me at my birth. It's hereditary. The cure for preeclampsia symptoms—high blood pressure and blinding migraine—is to deliver the baby.

Emerson and I look at each other in fear. She's too little—we're not ready! All we've got is the gender and a name. Finding out the baby would be a girl, we come up with "Annsley," after Emerson's Grandmother Anne. But as we talked over the name, Emerson ends up morphing it into "Ainsley" and it sounds right.

Over the course of the night I get shots to improve the baby's lung function if she is born too soon to breathe on her own. I'm also given medicine to stop the contractions. We get the contractions under control and then I'm in the hospital on bed rest for a week. During my stay, we get a tour of the neonatal intensive care unit (NICU) and are introduced to families who also have 29-weekers.

I look down at a tiny baby with transparent skin. I don't want my baby to look like I did, at 27 weeks in the NICU. I want her to be big and fat and full term. I get released home to more bed rest.

I am 34 weeks and four days along, and feeling my blood pressure rise, with a piercing migraine that makes me see stars. It's going to be a long night. I continue to check my blood pressure with the wrap and attached pump for home use. I keep ice on my head for the migraine. Nothing is helping. Finally, at 4 a.m., I wake up Emerson. We call the high-risk doc. He said that I know my body best, and it's time.

My mother's instinct tells me my baby is strong, but my body is failing to be a safe space for her to live before birth. When we get to the hospital, a nurse looks at me and says she will start a Pitocin drip, a medicine to induce labor. She said I could be in labor as long as three days. And I make my first decision as a mother.

"No, I'm having a C-section," I said. End of discussion.

"Don't you want to experience a natural birthing plan?" counters the nurse.

No, I don't want a birthing plan.

"No," I said, firmly. "I want a healthy baby."

At this point Ainsley is healthy and not stressed. If I'm in labor for three days trying to push her out, who knows what state she'll end up in. Much less, I do not have the strength to push for three days. The docs realize it's time for the baby to come out one way or another. They agree to the C-section.

"We can get you in at noon," says the doctor, like it's a reservation at a restaurant.

Ainsley Frances Scott is born at 12:42 p.m. March 8, 2011. Frances is a family name, after my grandmother, aunt and cousin.

It takes some oxygen and rubbing to turn her pink and hear her cry. My daughter's voice leaves no doubt that her lungs are strong.

"We woke her up from her nap and she was pouting," the doc reports.

In the recovery room, Emerson is watching me. I daze in and out of consciousness.

"Are you OK?" asks my husband.

"Yesssss," I respond, slurring my words.

"OK," he said. "I'm going to be with the baby." Now that's a plan.

I watch him walk away, then fall into a drug-induced sleep. I wake up every couple of hours, and Emerson checks in, telling me how cute our baby is, then goes back to her side. He is clear which of his girls need his primary attention that day, and I love him for it. I am out of the woods. Ainsley has just entered the noisy, dazzling forest outside of her mother.

Emerson is the first to hold her, feed her and change her, without hesitation. I am the one who is fearful of being able to support Ainsley enough to thrive. I have to break out of my history of struggling babies! I watch Emerson skillfully carry our little 4-pound, 6-ouncer gently in his arms, oxygen line trailing behind him to the NICU, like he is made to be a dad. He's got this; I can go back to sleep.

I hold her that evening in my wheelchair, asking for forgiveness.

"I'm sorry, baby, I'm sorry I couldn't keep you cookin' longer."

She looks up at me with her lavender blue eyes that say, *No worries, Mommy. You're a keeper.*

She spends two weeks in the unit, while every day I do not waver from my privileged maternal post: breast feeding, pumping breast milk to replenish the stock, going home for a nap, coming back in the evening, and repeat. A nurse calls us every night to report on her sleeping times and anything else we may have missed when I was at home. The nurses are wonderful partners getting Ainsley off to a good start.

But it takes me awhile to let go of the fear for her life. Whenever I enter the unit, I always brace myself for the worst. What if? Emerson helps to keep my fears at bay. I can count on him to give Ainsley what she needs.

Once we get her home, away from the machines that

monitor every danger, she looks ready to take on the job of being sweet and cuddly. Family members travel to Denver to see her. I begin to allow myself to feel like a competent mom, proud of the life we created, a life that would last.

CHAPTER 14

Sky of Terror

My mother's childbirths threaten her health, then she rallies several years, rising tall to the occasion of our March of Dimes travels in the limelight. But as I get older, the highs and lows of my mother's health is a scary ride for an only daughter.

One day the scary ride turns literal for my mom, while I am on the ground looking up in shock with the rest of the country on Sept. 11, 2001. Thousands of families are terrorized that day by the surreal spectacle of whole airplanes becoming lethal puppets to cut the World Trade Center at the knees, and bomb the Pentagon.

I'm a junior in high school, sitting in my history class when the planes hit. I'm terrified because my mom was flying out of Chicago to Washington that day for a meeting. Nervously, I go on to my next class and then get a call from the school office.

"Laura, your dad is in the office to pick you up," says my teacher.

Why? Why is he here when he's supposed to be at work? Mom!

When I spot him waiting for me in the office I try to read his face. My mom's plane, along with many others, had made an emergency landing. The pilots were taking orders from U.S. officials to land immediately once they realized that planes were being hijacked to attack the towers of commerce and the seat of the military.

My dad tells me if the planes did not land ASAP, they could be in jeopardy. My mother is safe; I am among the lucky. But I'm numb from the near-miss. We are very fortunate to face only the small worry of how to get Mom home from Oakbrook, Illinois, where her plane landed. Buses, trains and cars froze in fear of going anywhere. The what-ifs start.

What if she was on the other plane?

CHAPTER 15

Ambassador Encore

A year after 911, life has been reset for us, and I'm sitting at home having coffee with my mother when she gets a phone call.

"Laura would love to," chirps my smiling mother to whoever is calling.

What has she signed me up for now? Fox Sports News is sponsoring a sports awards event as a benefit for the March of Dimes. The gig involves posing for photos next to the premature infants at Loyola Medical, then giving a speech at a dress-up dinner to an audience of pro sports players and their fans. I'm not thrilled about going through a nerve-wracking speech, but it will be nice to visit the babies.

I have been out of the spotlight 11 years since my ambassador run. I'm in my senior year of high school, tan, blonde and the ambassador for myself. My life is my friends and my plans to go to college at Purdue to study child development. But the cause for premature babies never sleeps.

Mom and I go to Nordstrom to find the right fundraising outfit, trying on lots of skirts and blouses to impress the philanthropic world. I want to look my age, 17, but a mature 17. I have come a long way since I flubbed my first one-line speech at 6. We finally find a tan suede skirt and black top, with tall black boots.

I walk those boots into the hospital, almost a full-grown, healthy woman, standing tall in sharp contrast to the current batch of fragile babies, in the same room of incubators where I spent the beginning of my life. Some of the same nurses who had cared for me are still here. They smile and greet me with oohs and awes. They marvel at how big I am now, recalling the days when I was less than 2 pounds and they would lift me like a soft twig to change my tiny diaper. The nurses said they would have "dance parties" at the midnight feeding hour, cradling the premature infants in their arms and gliding them across the room, as if to woo them toward a life that would include such joys as dancing.

Draped in a yellow gown with gloves and a face mask, I slowly walk over to an incubator and look down. There is a tiny body with wires, tubes and tape all over. He was born at 29 weeks, giving him two weeks on me, when I was the one wired and taped at 27 weeks.

"The outlook looks good. He just needs to grow," says a nurse.

I place my hand next to him in the incubator; it's bigger than his little body. I watch his chest rise and fall as he tries to breathe on his own. When I look up, our photographer is capturing pictures of me next to my little cohort. This baby will make it. This little one has a chance, I tell myself. I am proof.

I remove my protective coverings and my mother and I leave the hospital into the bright sunny daylight. Mom is solemn and quiet.

"What are you thinking?" I ask.

She looks at me. "That was you. Now look at you. We made it!"

My English teacher had helped me prepare for my speech that night at the Fox Sports event downtown Chicago in a big ballroom. Every day on my lunch hour she coached me as I practiced my lines. I want to have the speech memorized to keep everyone's attention.

Walking into a huge, dark, beautiful room I am surrounded by men in suits and women in elegant dresses. The tables flicker with candles, and chandeliers are hanging from the ceiling. Video cameras are everywhere, and microphones are lined up across the stage.

Sitting at a gold-clothed round table, with my parents and other dignified looking guests, I give my mom a nervous look. When I was a 6-year-old ambassador, my mom did the talking on the stage.

"Do I have to go up there alone?"

"You'll be fine," she says. "Just remember what you practiced."

But suddenly my mind escapes the scene, and I forget why I'm here.

I am loudly reminded by the giant football player at the podium who is introducing me. I grab a glass of cold water, put down my napkin, smile weakly at my parents and take the stage. People are up on their feet clapping.

My speech goes well. But it feels like they are applauding for the wrong person. I want to tell them that I don't need to take a bow for simply living my life. In moments like this, though, my actual life is altered into a symbol—with the power that brings people to their feet. It means the work of the March of Dimes pays off. The applause is huge.

There is a clip of the Fox benefit on TV news and my friends are excited and proud of me. These events boost my self-confidence to speak in public. Learning how to hold an audience in my palm prepares me for a speech years later on the worst day of my life.

CHAPTER 16

The Pink Line

With the joy of Ainsley's arrival, I also grieve and pay homage to the first, short life that was once inside me. What would she or he have looked like?

Ainsley keeps us busy and we are not even thinking about another child. Until she is 16 months. Suddenly the idea of a sibling brightens our toy-covered living room like morning light. This time I long for a pregnancy to give my daughter what I had always wanted, a brother or sister. Emerson and I are her playmates, but we can't quite match a child's enthusiasm over the world's amazing discoveries that pop every day in her big, blinking eyes.

Months go by with lots of ovulation and pregnancy tests. Negative and negative, over again. I want to be pregnant so badly, I am practically delusional, staring at the test stick, thinking I see a positive sign in the little window.

One day I see an actual second pink line appear, crossing over the first line on the test stick. It's very faint but it's there. I FaceTime my mom.

"I have a surprise!"

She smiles into the camera.

"You're going to be a grandmother again."

She's beaming through my phone like magic.

Emerson and I are thrilled. We hug in the driveway after we get back from the doctor's office, and go out to dinner to celebrate.

Two weeks later the spark suddenly extinguishes itself. I have a terrible migraine the night before. The pain and blood this time are overwhelming, as my body closes the door on another someone I already loved.

With the first miscarriage, the D&C was necessary because my body doesn't reject the lifeless fetus on its own. But this time I can opt out of the D&C. This time I am a close-up witness of the loss of who could have been. For days, I watch the failed pregnancy bleed out, a natural yet emotionally excruciating, drawn-out death. I am draining inside out, leaving me a blurry ghost of joy.

After four years in Littleton, we start a new chapter and relocate from Colorado to Minnesota. It's an exciting move—my husband embarks on a career with his family's business, creating and distributing bright greeting cards in stores nationwide. We settle in the lovely small city of Stillwater, in the east Twin Cities metro along the St. Croix River, a national scenic waterway. I am happy to find a position as a preschool teacher.

CHAPTER 17

The Next Wife

My mom and dad have a good marriage. "I'm going to marry that man," Mom tells herself when she sees my father for the first time at the Freshman First Nighter at Purdue. She loves to tell me that romantic story. Three years after she spots him, they both end up presidents of their Greek houses and plan a sorority-fraternity mixer. David is late to the party. Candyce is about to leave when they meet in the stairwell.

They fall in love as she earns her degree in education, his in business. They are engaged in May of their senior year, and marry three months later. They love deeply. She is his cheerleader. He is her champion. They take care of each other.

They buy a comfortable two-story house in Naperville. She becomes a grant writer for the YMCA. He works for his family's office products business. They are happy at home and out in the world, using their talents. They enjoy a church community. My mother volunteers at church, as well as serving as a Brownie troop leader for the Girl Scouts. Plus she volunteers for a support group for mothers dealing with difficult pregnancies.

The marriage weathers their own pregnancy and newborn losses before I was born. They are grateful parents and build us a sturdy, three-member family. They teach Sunday School at church together, coach my soccer team together.

When I'm 10, my parents begin a tradition of family vacations on the warm beaches of South Carolina, a nourishing respite from the cold Chicago winters.

At 40, my mom starts getting sick a lot. She ends up spending whole winters in South Carolina. She keeps working despite her failing health, and buoys her spirits writing religious devotionals. She and I make it a mother-daughter project to eventually publish a collection of her writings.

She moves to South Carolina at age 53, and my father divides his time there and back in Naperville. Soon after

I get married, my parents sell my childhood home and relocate permanently to South Carolina.

She is grateful to be near the water. "The ocean can fix anything," she often says.

She is thrilled to become Ainsley's grandma and Ainsley worships her. Before she is old enough to be able say the word grandma, Ainsley calls her "Gaga." My mother is pleased to see Ainsley inspired by the ritual of prayer at a young age. She writes about the story of when Ainsley is 2, instructing the family in her own way to please pray, repeatedly, through dinner.

She has the idea that we must pray throughout the meal. So during the meal she announces "pay pease" and we comply.

When Ainsley is 4, my mother recalls, she captures her audience with a song about the Bible: "The B-I-B-L-E yes that is the book for me . . ." She takes a bow and my mom and I clap loudly. Mom is proud that Bible is the first word Ainsley learns to spell.

My father is a devoted care taker. *David has always taken care of me,* writes my mother, *since the first time he brought me a root beer at the Pi Phi House to staying by my side through all the babies and Laura.*

I know he understands every spectrum of me . . . I could go on and on about the many attributes I love about David, his laugh and sense of humor, his compassion, his business mind, his trust, his endurance, fortitude and perseverance, but the best thing about David is—he will continue to find me that perfect sunset!

Our family adopts Sunshine, a golden retriever, when I'm in grade school. We are dog people.

Sunny was technically Laura's dog, mom writes. Laura had a love/hate relationship with her. Sunny tormented her by stealing her gloves on the cold winter days or jumping on her as she screamed, "Mommy, get her off, I don't like this dog!"

But toward the end of Sunny's life, she was a constant comfort and loyal buddy particularly through Laura's kidney cancer and recovery—always by her side. Laura returned the favor to Sunny and was by her side when she was put to sleep.

David thinks Sunny is his dog, Mom's story continues. *He was the one who fed her every morning and "rough-housed" with her by playing tug-of-war.*

But I know that Sunny was my dog! I was the one who brushed her, talked to her and even had to hunt her down when she escaped from the yard. Since I work from my home, she was always at my feet, always listening attentively to my ranting about work or waiting for a gentle pat when my work was completed. On cold days she even kept my feet warm.

Just as Sunny is there for me while I went through cancer, later there is Moses, another of our golden retrievers, who is there for my mom as she struggles with her health. Mom writes about how Moses wakes her up with a wet kiss.

He is my happy-go-lucky guy. He is a lover boy, but frustration can abound when this "Big Guy" acts as if he is a defiant frat boy. As a puppy his big game was rolling in mud holes in the yard to the point of being incognito.

I cannot fail to the mention the moment when 15 minutes before a Christmas party, our golden decided to run around the yard like a bat out of Hades, dashing through the decorated bushes and coming out wearing the Christmas lights. There I stood in my silk party dress and high-heeled shoes trying to decide whether to cry or laugh. I chose the latter.

At age 57, Mom is tethered to a portable oxygen tank. At 59, she turns a frightening corner—rejected as a lung transplant candidate because her body is too weak. She is devastated by her prognosis of five years.

At 60, my mother's last year, I am flying from Minnesota to South Carolina every month to be with her, and some of our family's conversations feel dangerous to me.

"Make sure your next wife is a good Christian woman," Mom tells Dad, "and loves you as much as I do."

In her dying days, my mother throws out this life raft to my father. My dad does not refuse the kind gesture from his wife of 37 years. She is serious, but tries to keep the subject of his presumed second wife lighthearted.

"I know she will never compete with me," she jokes.

Ainsley is 5 when my mother is nearing the end. She loves her grandmother down to her toes.

"Ainsley will not call her Grandma," insists my mother. "Always remind her that I was her *first* grandma."

"I love you," Dad replies to Mom, ignoring her request.

But the thought of my dad being with another woman pierces me like adulterous betrayal. I can hardly bear losing my mother. The loss of their marriage will steal another primary source of love.

No! No, Dad. Don't think about replacing Mom! She doesn't really want you to marry someone else. She's just saying that to make it seem like her death won't be as bad as we think. Don't take away the foundation of my family. It's always been just the three of us. Don't pull out from under me the wobbly three-legged stool I am trying to keep standing on.

"Mom, come on," I say out loud. "You're right here!"

When Dad leaves the room, I am more direct. "Why do you keep talking to him about his next wife? You are still here," I remind her. Trying to convince myself she will always be my father's wife.

"He is going to get married again, Laura," says my mother, laying out the hard facts of the crime.

"He can't be alone," she says, case closed.

He won't be alone! He'll still have me!

"And you have to be OK with it."

I won't be OK, Mom. Please. Don't die.

Later, I concede to myself that my mother was giving my father a gift. It was not my gift to reject. I allow a small crack of light to come through death's door. One day my father might be happy without her. But I don't have to think about that now.

CHAPTER 18

Letters

Mom and I are on the couch under a blanket together. Outside, there's a crisp breeze weaving through the September air. Inside, there's the chill of dread threading down my spine, knowing it's a matter of months when I'll lose this person beside me. I try bargaining with God for more time.

"You know Ainsley is starting kindergarten next year, Mom. Who am I going to call when I send her off the first day?"

"Your father," she says, problem solved.

"I'm going to miss you so much." I start to sob into her shoulder.

"I just hope that I have taught you all that you need to be successful in this life," she says. It sounds like the official line all good parents should recite to their children. But tears are in her voice.

My head on her shoulder, I ask for something doable. Something that does not require an act of God.

"Would you write letters to Ainsley?"

My mom is a writer. It doesn't occur to me that I'm asking for something that would be difficult for her. I need her to leave these letters for my daughter, and for me.

She pulls back from me, startled.

"What? What do you mean letters? Do I have to?"

"Mom, it will help her—us—remember you. She can learn all about you even when you are not here."

Writing her life stories, framed by religious inspiration, is one thing. But writing in the more direct voice of a personal letter hits a nerve.

"I don't know Laura, that sounds hard for me. I won't know her when she is 8, 13 and 16. I won't know what her interests will be, or her wants in life. It makes me too sad."

"She will want to read them."

Mom finally consents and writes a few letters to 5-year-old Ainsley. And she stays alive long enough for her granddaughter to receive them.

Ainsley practices her new reading skills, reading the letters aloud to her grandmother.

My Dearest Ainsley,

As I write this I am sad, because I will not know the little girl you have grown up to be. I want to tell you more things about my childhood. I learned from my mistakes.

I enjoyed playing with friends. We played hopscotch, tag, jump rope and dolls.

I joined Brownies-Girl Scouts. We met every Saturday and I was chosen leader of the troop.

I loved to read and read many Bible stories. I have included a few of my favorites for you to share with your mom and dad. I memorized a couple too. The first one was John 3:16—For God so loved the world . . . and 23 Psalm, Remember that God and Jesus love you because you are special.

Keep the love from Gaga in your heart too. Always wear a smile, it looks pretty on your face.

I love you forever,

Gaga

CHAPTER 19

Lavender

Like a secret, it's the scent my mother and I share in her final stretch of life. It is my honor to take care of her when she no longer can care for herself. I feed her, dress her, bathe her, and tuck her in bed.

"It's time to go to the spa, Mom," I say at bedtime, cheerful.

I am inviting her to take a break from the sorrowful job of waiting to die. I open a bottle of lavender lotion and massage it into her bruised skinny legs. The scent from Earth's garden ushers us back into the realm of living. For a few minutes.

"It feels so good," says my mother, giving me a tired smile.

Then I brush her teeth, plug in sounds from nature on her iPad, and crawl into bed next to her. I lay my head on her chest listening for and feeling the movement of her breath.

My dad comes into the room to say his good nights. "What was the happiest part of your day?" he asks her. It's their bedtime routine.

Mom nods toward me. "Laura is here."

Then my father kisses her forehead.

"I love you more than you will ever know," she tells him.

"I will miss you so much," I tell her, hugging her little frame tight.

I hold her hand, and remember the story she tells of when I am living in an incubator. She can't yet hold me, but through the holes in the incubator she puts her finger in my tiny palm. Throughout the rest of her life, holding hands is our thing.

One night when I'm a young girl, a storm is noisy with unrelenting thunder and bright, eerie lightning. "Mom, can I come in and lay in bed with you?"

Laura never liked storms, and so many times she would end up in my room to ride the storm out, Mom writes. *Laura and I lay there, and I held her hand. We didn't say much to each other as our hands and hearts did all the talking.*

I began thinking about all the times I had held her hand, beginning in the hospital, holding micro-tiny premature hands with tiny spaghetti-like fingers that barely wrapped around my little finger. I thought about all the other storms and joys of her life: struggling with her academics in high school but making Dean's List at Purdue, disagreements with friends but making new friends at Purdue and of course the broken romances that brought so many tears.

On the long nights when she was diagnosed with kidney cancer and the recovery after surgery—how she clung to my hand for strength and support. Little did she realize she was the very one I was clinging to for my strength and support.

Laura let go of my hand, and as she did, it occurred to me that I may never have to hold her hand again through a thunderstorm. Emerson will be the one to hold her hand through all the storms of her life.

"Laura, you will have to grieve me. It will be the hardest thing you do—but you'll have to do it."

I am the one taking care of her now, but my mother is still being my mother, giving me advice. And giving my dad and I permission to live past her.

CHAPTER 20

Urgent Prayer

The last days of my mother's life replay like an unending loop. On the Monday after Easter, she doesn't call or text me. It's unusual because we always talk every morning and throughout the day, no matter how sick she is. I try calling her; the phone goes ringing and ringing in my ears. I start to sweat and my stomach ties itself in a knot. Is she not answering because she's dead?

Finally she picks up my call, in a small, frail voice on the other end. "Hi, baby."

I know that means she isn't feeling well. Whenever she feels bad she speaks to me as if I am a child. She tells me she wants me to remember her "mothering." We talk, and she says she is just resting her heart today. She sounds distant and drugged up, not herself. I don't buy her "just resting" line. What if this is her last day? I am choking with anxiety.

When I'm low, Mom says, "Get up, get dressed and put your makeup on—you will feel better." She follows her own advice even in the final days, applying blush to her cheeks, some mascara and classic red lipstick, and gets her short blonde hair washed. Looking presentable, hair brushed and blow dried, makes her feel as comfortable as she can. That Monday she doesn't do her makeup or brush her hair. But I have to, to get ready for work.

The week drags on in dread. On Wednesday morning my daughter gets a surprise in the mail from my mother. It is a small white chef coat and hat she can wear to practice her cooking and baking. We take a picture and text it to my mom at 6:52 a.m. My phone tells me the text was "read" but there is no reply.

I go to work at my preschool, trying to distract myself with the children's laughter and stories. But I know something isn't right. At 9 a.m. I call my mother's daytime caregiver. As soon as she hears my voice on the line, she says, in her big Southern accent, "You get comin', ya hear? Get on a flight and get here."

"How much time do I have? Do I have until tomorrow?"

"Yes, I think so."

My mind is spinning like flashing siren lights. I hear people talking to me, but I can't understand what they are saying. Everything is a blur. I begin to shake and my skin gets really cold. I want to run and hide. This is the moment that I have dreaded since I was 12 years old, when my mom becomes seriously sick; she is not going to bounce back like she has so many times before. This is it.

I call my father at work. He is the strong head of the household, the nondramatic one. The practical one.

"Let's not get ahead of ourselves," he said. "Let's see what she does in the next couple hours."

I fall to the cold tile floor in the break room and crumple into a ball, trying to make myself as small as I can. "It's happening, it's happening and I'm not ready!" I burst into tears, sobbing alone on the tiny kitchenette floor of the preschool.

Then I jerk myself up and run to hug my daughter, just a few doors down in the same preschool building. She always carries the presence of God. She knows what I need, hugging me tight.

"I love you, Mommy." Oh, how I want to say that to my own mother and hug her tight.

In the next couple of hours there are phone calls back and forth from me to the caregiver to my father. But I need to hear my mom's voice. I thought from her tone I would be able to tell how much longer I have with her.

Mom still wants to be my mother. She gets on the phone and asks me about work, her granddaughter, the weather. I don't want to act like everything is fine.

I picture her lying in bed, getting drops of morphine and sedating medicine, calming her, helping her breathe easier. I know the oxygen is turned up full blast, as she tries to speak to me in a strong voice. I know their 100-pound golden retriever, Moses, is a comfort at her feet. I book a flight to South Carolina for 6 a.m. the next morning. How I hope I can get there before she's gone.

When I get home from work, my mother and I have another phone call, using FaceTime to see each other. But the meds are confusing her and my dad has to tell her it's me on the phone. He holds the phone close to her face and I see them cuddle together for the last time. My mother's face is swollen and her voice sounds funny. Her breath is labored and her mouth is dry.

"Mom, I'm coming to see you tomorrow."

Hearing this, she smiles ear to ear, and looks at my dad to confirm it was true. He nods. I'll never forget the joyful look on her face in that moment.

"Well, how long are you going to stay?" she asks, in true Mom fashion.

I bite my tongue. *Until you die.* "For a while," I tell her.

"Tell Laura you love her," Dad says to my mother.

"I love you, baby," she says with a brief smile.

"I love you, too."

My father puts my mother to bed at 9 p.m., resting peacefully, breathing through her oxygen tubes. My father goes to bed shortly after, but tries to keep an ear open, listening for anything my mom might need from him. He finally drifts to sleep, but at midnight is awakened by the frightening sound of my mother gasping for air. Her oxygen level has dropped down to 30 percent.

He calls her caregiver who had gone home for the night; she comes back right away. I get a text message at 1:15 a.m. that the nurse, the caregiver, and my father are attending to her, and that they would call soon.

If this is Mom's time, Lord, take her. Please don't let her suffer.

My phone rings again at 3:12 a.m. I see "Dad" on the screen.

"NO! NO!" I scream. Shaking, I pick up the call.

"*No*," I command, "don't tell me."

"Your mom tried to wait to see you, but it just got too hard. It was too hard for her. She loved you very much."

CHAPTER 21

Holding Hands

The bond between my dad and I is magnified by my mother being sick so much of my childhood. We stumble along a path that we know, in the foreseeable future, leads to burying her together. We both carry a picture in our pockets of our little family down to just the two of us.

I am forever grateful we have each other those few days after my mother dies. We are alone in the house grieving her. Behind closed doors, we allow each other raw anger and weeping to spill in the dark hours.

In the days before the funeral, our loved ones come around. They thread their healing into the cloth that clothes the two of us, as we are strangely still living and talking in the empty space where my mother should be.

At the funeral home, my dad and I are sitting in the parking lot. I look at him.

"This is it. This is the moment we have been dreading for 15 years."

"I know," says Dad. "We can do it together."

Inside the funeral chapel, we hover a safe distance away from the open casket. I am scared. When we finally reach the casket, I collapse in my father's arms, shocked by the finality. Only her quiet body is in there. My mom is elsewhere. She has been ushered permanently into memory.

My father holds me. "She is OK, Laura." She is no longer suffering.

I touch my mother's hands. It's another surprise. "They are still soft."

I expected death, the uninvited guest, to have quickly erected a cold wall between itself and the living. But it does not stand in the way of the body's last tangible gesture of comfort. I hold my mother's hands as my father holds me.

This is the last time that it will be just the three of us, I tell myself. *Now it's just the two of us, Dad.*

My father turns to the funeral director. "Thank you. This was important to Laura."

For my mother's service, I have to stand in front of the

people who have gathered to say goodbye to her. Before I get up to speak, I turn to my dad.

"How am I going to do this?"

He remembers all those times I am in front of an audience, with a microphone, telling people how the March of Dimes saved me.

"You've done this before," he says. But this time no one is clapping.

CHAPTER 22

Dad and Me

My father has always been my biggest supporter. He is the first to lay eyes on me, to touch my tiny hand, and to hear my cry.

We play tennis together, and basketball in the driveway. He catches and throws a ball between us for hours, as I talk his ear off about whatever happened to me that day. He listens.

My dad and I stay close as I get older. There are times my mother is jealous of all the attention I receive from him. When he comes home from work, he and I often take a walk, leaving my mom at home. He can see my point of view in almost any situation.

Growing up, my mom and I sometimes succumb to a hot and cold mother-daughter relationship. The dinner table quickly becomes a stage for arguments about petty things. I accuse her of looking at me the wrong way.

"What are you staring at?" I demand, gritting my teeth.

"You, you are sitting across the table from me, where else am I supposed to look?" she snaps back.

My father silently stands up and moves his and my mother's plates to switch places, so Mom and I are no longer sitting directly across from each other. He is the peacekeeper between two strong females. Yet I always feel like he chooses my side over my mother's in an argument.

It's after dark on the Purdue campus. I am driving to a party and get lost. I call Dad in the middle of the night.

"Where is the Sigma Chi house?"

"Laura, where are you?" my father asks, concerned. He talks me safely onto the route toward my destination. "Be sure to call me when you get there—I won't go to sleep."

I call back when I arrive at the frat house.

"Have fun, Sweetie," says my wonderful dad.

If I ever need him to help me through something, he always comes to me or is there over the phone.

On my wedding day, my dad and I almost steal the show. The minister asks who gives this woman away. My father holds my arm tight.

"Her mother and I do," he says, flushed and proud.

This is his cue to let go of me to reach Emerson at the altar. But my dad and I lock into a hug that lasts so long Emerson starts to wonder if the "giving away" is going to happen. He thinks it's my dad not letting go of me, but I am the one who can't let go just yet.

CHAPTER 23

A Date

It's 10 weeks after my mother's death and I get a call from my father in South Carolina. I see his name pop up on my phone for FaceTime and smile. I miss my mother. And, living in Minnesota, I miss my dad because he's far away. I miss my family and want to be near to him. I hate that we live so far apart while we both grieve my mother.

"What are you doing?" I ask him, bright as possible.

"Well, I actually just got back from a date!" he says, sheepish.

"WHAT? With *who*?" I am shocked.

"The hospice program coordinator. She called and wanted to get coffee and I thought what the heck!"

Double shock. My mother's *hospice coordinator*?

"Did you like it? Do you like her?" Holding it together. Just.

"I don't know, I think so. I thought she was calling to suggest a follow-up appointment after your mom. But the more we talked, the more we clicked and liked each other. She's going to come by this weekend."

"I'm happy for you," I lie. "Love you. I gotta go."

I hang up the phone and cry.

This is proof. Mom is gone. Living a long distance away has made it easy to fool myself that I just haven't seen her in a while. She is fine. Now my blinder is yanked off. She's dead. Another woman is in her shoes.

Actually, the hardest part is thinking of another woman in my mother's house with my mother's things, her decorating, her stuff. Our stuff. Our times together.

Nine months after Mom dies, my father comes to Minnesota for the first Christmas without her. He's with his girlfriend. I am in the kitchen doing dishes when I overhear him in the living room tell another woman he loves her. Seeing them together I can tell they are in love. I just didn't think I would hear it firsthand.

The following year, a week before Christmas, Dad tells me he has proposed, and they are getting married in July. I'm still in shock. He tells me that nothing can replace my mother, but his fiancée is a good companion to him. I want him to be happy, but I want my mom back, want us to be a family again. I have lost my sense of my place in the world. I am my mom and dad's daughter. But where is Mom?

Like an astronaut losing the tether to the mother ship, I am losing my father to this new woman. My family will never be the same. One of us is gone and the other has a new relationship. I am dangling in space alone with the story of my origin.

My mother was my person. I have my own family now, a husband and daughter I love. But my soul is aching for the heroine who carried me into this fragile world.

"You have your dad," Mom told me. "Make sure to tell him you love him when you see him."

I try to do that. Yet he has broken my heart. I'm a 33-year-old wife and mother. It isn't his fault, my adult self is telling the little girl in me who is motherless. But she is resisting. I am no longer No. 1 in his life.

I think about my absent sister and brother. My sister was my parents' first child, born at 32 weeks stillborn. Anna. The following year my brother, Joseph, is born and lives just a few hours. My dad gets to hold him. My mother is too sick from the childbirth to be able to hold him, regretting that he wasn't pulled out sooner.

My whole life my parents talk about Anna and Joseph like they are still alive. On family vacations, when I bring along friends as travel companions instead of siblings, my mom wants to tell their birth stories.

I want my siblings with me now to grieve our mother together. My sister and brother are buried in a mausoleum with my mother's parents, in my mom's hometown of Rushville, Indiana. Anna is in the same crypt with my grandfather. Eight months before my mother dies, my grandmother dies. Joseph's little casket is relocated into the same crypt with my grandma.

Only my dad and I know the intimate moments of losing my mother. We have the same hole in our lives. This is our bond. How far can it stretch?

Where is the lavender? Oh, God. I can't feel her hand in mine. It's memory. It's not enough.

CHAPTER 24

Last Egg in the Basket

After our second miscarriage, we keep trying. And then turn to medical technology. We meet with a doctor about in vitro fertilization (IVF), when the egg is removed from the woman and joined with sperm in a lab to create an embryo. The embryo then is inserted in the woman's uterus. But the doctor tells us that the scar tissue I have inside from endometriosis makes this process too difficult.

So we decide to attempt intrauterine insemination (IUI), in which sperm is medically inserted directly into the woman's uterus to meet the egg.

All of it feels wrong. I am an anxious mess the morning of my IUI, not able to sleep the night before. But I'm not turning back. I look at the doc.

"Let's do this."

It starts with an internal ultrasound. Then the tech gets the same look in her face I have seen before.

"I'll be right back," she says.

The doctor comes back in the room. "We cannot continue with the procedure today, you have too many cysts on your ovaries."

I can't accept this. "No, I'm mentally ready now. We have to do it."

The doctor refuses. We have to wait another long month to attempt another IUI. When that doesn't work we finally stop trying. After losing my mother this year, I can't handle another loss of a would-be child.

The next year I lose my embattled uterus to a hysterectomy. However, we choose a hysterectomy that leaves one ovary for a future IVF with a surrogate mother, if we can find such a generous woman.

The next year the ovary gets tangled in the bowel, and I need emergency surgery to remove it.

CHAPTER 25

The Art of Listening

My body often has been on shaky ground. But my marriage always feels solid. Over the years we've mastered the tricky art of listening to each other. I feel heard and he feels heard, and that has locked in a lasting partnership.

If there's a conflict, we give each other turns to talk, with an understanding that we don't have to be defensive. If someone gets defensive, we give each other space to process the conflict, then come together again to do the process until it works.

This marital tool is pulled off the shelf after a weekend when we travel from Minnesota to Indiana, for a gathering at a rented cottage on a lake with my father, his fiancée and my cousins. Ainsley loves playing with her cousins, going swimming. They bring her gifts. Our 6-year-old daughter tells us the lady with her grandfather is nice.

My dad tells me he does not envision this woman as my stepmother, he just wants her to be accepted as his wife. I am overwhelmed in the strange new family dynamic with this woman in the picture, not long after my mother's death.

On the way home I am in a silent stew, feeling defensive. Emerson gives me the space I need. Later we talk and process our feelings. At the beginning of our marriage, we are clumsy in times of strain, but we take the time to create a safe and loving experience as wife and husband.

We are a team. Sometimes Ainsley tries to play the Mom vs. Dad card, and hits the team wall. She despairs to her dad when Mom won't let her do something. Dad may admit that something she wants is OK with him, but if Mom says no, then it's no.

"Why do you always have to be on the same team?" Ainsley wails.

We get Ainsley someone to be on her side all the time—another Springer Spaniel puppy. And it's a score for the team.

CHAPTER 26

Invisible

As a young girl I attend Sunday school at our Methodist church, but I don't find God there. As a teenager I transition from Sunday school to the Sunday service, sitting between my parents, my mom's arm around me tight. I am safe and loved inside the sanctuary of stained glass windows and wooden pews, but I don't notice God milling around anywhere.

My mother worries about me. She sets up a talk for me and the minister, to discuss my doubts and questions. The minister is tall and big, with a voice even bigger. My mom sometimes tears up as he's preaching with the passion of the Lord speaking through him.

I sit in a big wing armchair across from the minister, who looks huge behind his big wooden desk.

"Why do I have to believe in God?"

"You don't have to, but God would like a relationship with you. That's all He's asking for is a relationship."

He listens to my doubts and doesn't argue with me, but before we part he says, with confidence, "Trust and have faith and you will see God work in your life."

I am not convinced.

Not long after, my dad and I go to South Dakota with a youth group from our church to work on homes needing repair, and volunteer at a soup kitchen. I do it to please my dad and the minister. My first friend Genny, who I've known since kindergarten, is with our group and I like the talks with her and the other teenagers on our trip; I'm curious what other people think about God. Sometimes the God believers make sense. But not always.

One sunny early morning we are packing up to move to another campsite, but I don't feel like helping. I find a beat-up picnic bench in the middle of some trees, where no one else is around. One of the youth counselors finds me.

"Why don't you believe in God? What don't you understand about Him?"

"I'm confused. I can't think about something I can't see."

The counselor gives me a challenge. "Look up into the sky and say a prayer to ask God to come into your life."

I roll my eyes. "OK."

People say they feel God's presence and I used to be someone who thought that was crazy. But I look up at the blue sky that day and suddenly feel peaceful and in control. I give the counselor a look.

"God is here," he says. "You just have to believe, trust and have faith."

It doesn't sound crazy anymore because, without seeing, I am noticing all the ways God works in my life.

As an adult, there are times that I believe in God, but it feels like He's on the other side of the world. At 31, I take myself to church one morning looking for God's light to filter through the dark hour I'm in. There's a baptism service going on but I don't see how it has anything to do with me. I was already baptized as a baby. I'll just listen to the music and go home.

Then the pastor invites all of us to baptism, and it sounds like he's talking about people who would be baptized for the first time, or anyone due for a renewal policy with God. I feel the Holy Spirit take my hand and walk me up to the podium. Someone offers me some dry clothes to change into after the plunge.

Climbing three steps, I take the hand of my pastor. He leads me into a waist high pool, puts his hands on my shoulders and asks if Jesus Christ is my Lord and Savior. Yes, I answer, slowly lowering into the pool. As I come up from the cool water people are clapping. There is joy in my soul. God is present again and does not forsake me.

CHAPTER 27

God's Hand

I find myself looking at my hand—the hand of cards from God. Some days I only see spades, the symbol associated with wisdom and death. Sometimes the hand is full of jokers. Some days I see hearts. How am I to play this hand?

At this writing I am 34. I want some kind of accounting of the losses, and fortunes, that have accumulated in my relatively young life. I want a sum of it all, translated into a language I understand, that rises above the daily noise of life. I want agency with God, to name His cards, to deal a win-win for me and this beautiful and terrible world.

Dear God,

Here are my cards. My wins and losses. Is there a way to interpret them, something I'm missing?

Yours,

Laura

My survival after birth, odds against me, is a card of triumph, a diamond out of the rocks. The triumph card shows up again, in my 23rd year, when cancer costs me a kidney but spares my life.

At 25 I am winning big when I marry a man among men, making vows of sickness and health even before he gets to the altar.

Only months later, I am living in a house of cards, in a frightening déjà vu of my parents' history when they tried to start a family. Thank God I do not end up holding two full-bodied newborns, their life stolen out of them. I don't see the faces of death in my miscarriages, but I witness their substance leaving me, drowning in bowls of blood.

In between these losses, Ainsley emerges from the treacherous travel through the womb, another diamond. I am a new mother at 27.

At 31, I lose the hand when my mother and best friend dies on April Fools' Day. Her death lands in the same week of the due date of the baby who dissolved in my second miscarriage. This round feels like the joker hiding in the deck, laughing at my worthless calendar.

When my uterus is removed, I play my last family

card by saving one ovary inside me. At 33, the ovary gets sick and I am rushed to the hospital to get it out before it kills me.

We all carry significant numbers in our lives, numbers that represent a story. My stand-out number is eight. Eight times I submitted to the surgeon's knife. It is a sum I use to wrap all the times I've been on the sterile table into one succinct portrayal of bodily endurance.

My gut passes the numbers one through eight, from one cut-out piece of my body to the next, like a white and red flag, torn but waving: 1) kidney; 2) miscarriage; 3) C-section; 4) endometriosis removal (during which the knife nicks my bowel, requiring a colostomy bag for six weeks); 5) bowel reconstruction; 6) more endometriosis cut away, causing a raging infection; 7) hysterectomy due to the cysts and endometriosis invading my uterus; 8) my last ovary. (And, while they're in the neighborhood, my appendix is taken out during the same surgery.)

No. 8 and holding. No. 8 is down, but gets back up. No. 8 walks off the field, rips off the jersey, hollowed out, cursing, undefeated.

If this was a numbers game, the losses appear to add up more than the wins. But each win upstages the losing hand: I am a healthy survivor, a lucky wife and mother. I lost my mother too soon but I'm always grateful for the time I had with her, and my father's love abides. I'm working in my chosen field teaching preschool. I'm a certified massage therapist for babies to boot, massaging away aches and pains for my little clients.

Where to put the losses and wins? The losses are in a memory box that rumbles but keeps its lid on. The wins, on the other hand, are not contained; Emerson and Ainsley and my students win me over day after day.

Sometimes I'm angry at my hand, but most days I thank God for my life. Some days I want to ask Him if there is something more I should be doing besides marching for dimes, loving my family and friends, and inspiring other people's children as their teacher.

In conversations with my soul, I have come to understand that I need to lean on God, let go, and let myself breathe in His caring presence. I know I'll face more loss, yet I don't have to live in fear of loss. I am not a marked target. I am allowed to simply feel blessed for the love in my life and my sense of purpose in family and work. My presence and stories of loss, survival and gratitude are what I have to give to the world, just as God is a gift to me. There is a holy balance to that.

CHAPTER 28

Ocean Blue

There are always those things you wish you could have done, when the window was still open to do them. My mother was writing her own kind of memoir in her last year, with hopes it would become a book. In the year following her death, I publish it. I wish she could have held it in her own hands. But I honored her by binding the collection of her inspirational essays, to get into the hands of those who loved her, and for others who come across it and come to know this woman who welcomed God with strength inside vulnerability.

I have shared some of her passages earlier. This chapter is to open the window a bit more to *The Waters of My Soul,* by Candyce Krumwiede. I want you, dear reader, to know her.

The setting for her writing is Seabrook Island, a small town on the enchanting south coast of South Carolina, along the Atlantic Ocean. She rents a condo with a beach view. She stays near the water to clear her lungs and feel alive again. She "winters" there until a few years later when her husband permanently moves onto Seabrook Island.

I truly believe that God spoke loudly to me during my time on Seabrook Island, writes my mother, in the foreword.

In the chapter called "The Man and the Ocean," she adores her dad, as I adore mine, and credits him for introducing her to the sea.

The ocean winds called to him every summer. So he packed his beautiful wife and his precious little girls [two of them] *into the ol' Chevy, and off they went to the beach.*

Oh my, how he loved the ocean, and it saddens me that he will never know that I returned to the ocean to live my final days.

Mom writes about her first 13 years growing up on a farm in Indiana.

I showed sheep and horses in 4-H, loved dressing up my rabbits in dolls' clothes and spent so many hot afternoons in the haymow reading my books. My favorite time though was taking my two collies, Sandy and Lassie, and walking the bank of the Big Flat Rock River.

She loses her dad too soon, as I lose her, from the same lung disease that kills them both.

The spring of my seventh grade year my father died, and we sold the farm and moved to a subdivision. No longer did I have my outdoor haven to remind me of God's love and grace.

In her new outdoor retreat as an adult, Mom intently notices her surroundings, such as the shorebirds on Seabrook Island.

The pelicans often dive into water for their catch as if they are bomber planes. Then there are the gulls who just continue laughing as if they have some joke on you.

She singles out the "one-legged sanderling" in particular, wondering how he lost the leg and admiring how he goes on despite his "disability."

There he was hopping along the shore and running with the rest of the flock, not missing the timing of the surf coming in and going out.

I smile at the chapter called "The iPod"—I am responsible for her having this new piece of tech on her, on the otherwise unplugged shoreline, where she takes daily walks or jogs as long as she can.

One day I decided that I needed to "pick up the pace" of my jog on the beach so I plugged into my ears my iPod and braced myself for the music that my daughter had chosen for me. The first song that blasted in my ears was "Living on a Prayer" by Bon Jovi—wow—immediately my pace picked up as I soaked in the lively and exhilarating beat.

Bon Jovi's prayer within a song inspires her to thank God for "the magnificent world . . . and the promise of life anew."

I have mentioned we are dog people. Mom loves her own dogs, and practically every other dog that passes her way.

His ears were flapping in the gentle wind as the old red pickup truck sped by me . . . It made me laugh to see that big red bloodhound positioned perfectly in the bed of the truck, sniffing the marsh air like he was "King of the Wind."

In addition to birds, dogs and various creatures, Mom makes other friends during her residence by the sea.

Today is a full moon, and on Seabrook Island when there is a full moon, the island residents host a "Full Moon

Party." *Everyone gathers on the beach to watch the sun go down and moon rise . . . Have you ever considered the hospitality of God? He hosts a magnificent party every night as He turns on the lights . . .*

Throughout her book, my mother frames each day-to-day event within God's big picture, which never fails to uplift her. When she is mourning the death of her favorite cousin Susan, she takes her grieving to the shore.

I notice the dolphins jumping out of the water, playing like I have never seen before. It is as if they are performing a celebratory dance—a reminder that in death there is glory.

Like me, my mother also adores her mother, and brings her into the story like a mysterious, colorful new character in a play.

Her knees are so feeble, and her hips do not squarely fit her body, causing her gait to be slow and even laborious. She knows the challenge it will be to walk down the wooden steps for a beach walk . . . She wants so much to stroll down the beach one more time. So she flops her "red hat" upon her head for protection from the sun, carefully then places her body into the convertible, and the crew speeds toward the beach.

The beach walk is accomplished, and the old lady returns to the cottage with a smile on her face and the satisfaction that she has walked the beach, stairs and all.

The woman places her red hat on the hat rack, never again to wear it but leaving it behind as a symbol of determination, true grit and courage. This is how my mother has lived her whole life, writes my mom, stealing lines out of my mouth.

CHAPTER 29

The Picture

My mother is gone but her memory is fresh enough to touch like warm skin after a swim. She is living in me. She feels so near, how is it possible that my father is going to replace her this soon with a new wife?

The wedding day creeps closer. It prods me in the back like a big stick, walking toward a cliff. My parents' marriage and our close family of three is toppling over, splintering on the unforgiving rocks below.

I imagine my dad making vows to another woman, spoken lines that ink over the 37 years of my parents' marriage. And it's harder to bear because this woman is no stranger. She is someone my mother loved in her last seven months and how could she not? This woman oversaw my mother's hospice caretakers. That was her job and she did it well. My mother's dying days were softened by the competent work of a woman who would quickly fall in love with her husband.

Dying and hospice is extremely intimate business. But this feels too intimate. It's claustrophobic. My father's bride is privy to my family's private moments with death. We are grateful for the hospice care, yet are they not people who would attend this intimacy and then walk away from our lives, maintaining a kind of confidentiality of what they shared with us, like a therapist or pastor? They would leave my dad and I with our private experience intact.

What's wrong with this picture?

Well, I'm a grown woman and can't be so naive to not concede that love is always messy. It doesn't stay inside the lines we try to draw around our lives.

"I was happily married to your mother and I plan to be happily married again," says my dad, making it sound simple. What don't I understand about this equation?

"Take this as a compliment to your mother who I loved so deeply, and enjoyed it so much, I just want to do it over again."

It's a beautiful wedding. My first thought is Mom would have loved this. Someone is smiling at this thought.

OK, it's me. We can hear the ocean waves crashing, complementing the scent of the flowers at the altar. It's a hot day in the south, the sun is shining, pelicans are flying overhead in groups of 13, my father's favorite number. Of course.

I am in the first row. Behind me the cellist and violinist are playing traditional wedding songs. I want to run. But I look at my father in his navy blue suit, accented with an orange and blue tie, waiting for the bride to appear, as excited as a first-time young bridegroom. He is beaming. I am not in the picture at this moment. Yeah, but, it *is* a pretty picture.

Dad's smile gets bigger. I turn and there is my daughter making her way down the aisle as the flower girl. Her 7-year-old self is thinking this is the best job in the world—she gets to wear a pretty dress, with her hair done, and throw pretty flowers as she walks toward her grandpa.

But she is missing her grandmother more than we know. She's always telling me Gaga is with her in bed, and at school when she has no one to play with. She doesn't want her grandpa to forget her Gaga, but she is happy to do this special job today. At the end of the aisle she gives my dad a hug, and they both wait for the bride.

Ainsley loves watching her walk down the aisle, loves her white, lacy dress, how pretty and flowing it is. The bride hands her bouquet to Ainsley and she is thrilled with her *new* wedding job.

Is my dad reciting the same vows he did to my mother? Is he frightened, just a little, to promise 'til death do us part, again? Could he go through another parting at a deathbed? Or does it all feel brand new, a shiny suitcase on a newly discovered island that he can't wait to unpack.

I will hang on until this scary ride down the waterfall is over, tell myself these vows do not undo the vows he took with my mother. When my dad gets to heaven, my mom's love will be waiting for him.

Finally they are announced husband and wife. I stop spinning and smile and clap, grabbing my husband's hand. He leans into me.

"Go to the bathroom and take a minute," he whispers. "When you come back you'll feel better."

I didn't notice I was crying—shoulders shaking, tears streaming down my face crying. I want my first family back, Mom, Dad and me. I don't know what boat I just fell into. What does my family look like now?

Inside the bathroom the cool air conditioning hits my hot face with relief. My shoulders stop shaking and the tears are subsiding.

Mom, he's happy, I tell her, looking up in the mirror. *But we miss you.*

Peace reaches down to touch me. I made it through the wedding, and my mom is still with me. I splash water on my face and walk back out into the 100-degree South Carolina heat. I hug my father and his wife and give them my congratulations. I'm still not in the picture. But it's still a pretty picture.

An Afterword
How the Dimes Add Up

Lessons from the March of Dimes

I am the one in the blue sash, like a pretty 1st Place prize winner at the fair. I am the lucky, healthy preemie. When she's not in high heels on a stage with me, my mom is the one in boots on the ground, campaigning for the unlucky ones, to prevent the often crippling or fatal consequences of premature birth. She ends up running the Illinois March of Dimes campaign to promote healthy prenatal and pre-pregnancy practices—to prevent babies from being born, or even conceived, before it's safe.

"I think it's very important that the word gets out that prenatal care is very important, and prenatal care starts even before you think about pregnancy," says my mom, quoted in *The Naperville Sun*. "For young girls, it's taking care of their bodies and eating right."

As a post-child ambassador, I want to recognize the March of Dimes with a few words about their research and guidelines for bringing healthy children into the world.

Premature birth statistics

The preterm birth rate in the United States has worsened for a third year at this writing, rising to 9.93 percent in 2017, according to March of Dimes research. Premature infants are almost 20 times as likely as other infants to die in the first year of life. Premature babies who survive may suffer lifelong consequences, including developmental disabilities, blindness, chronic lung disease, cerebral palsy and other disabling conditions.

Women without health insurance often do not get prenatal care and are much more likely to deliver prematurely. Their babies are at a much higher risk of infant death.

In addition to the human toll, the societal cost of premature birth is more than $26 billion per year. Employers pay 12 times as much in health care costs for premature/low birthweight babies compared to babies born without these complications.

Delaying pregnancy until you're ready

Every two minutes in the U.S. a baby is born to a teen mother. About half the births in the United States are paid for by Medicaid, which primarily serves single, impoverished adults and children.

The March of Dimes guidelines urge potential parents to prevent pregnancies through birth control methods or abstinence, until they are healthy and ready to provide the 24-hour care every baby needs, and ongoing care and support throughout childhood.

Reducing the risk of premature birth

Before and after a pregnancy begins, the March of Dimes endorses the following life choices for would-be parents:

Vitamins: Take B9 vitamins, also known as folic acid or folate vitamins, or prenatal vitamins, which are available over the counter or by prescription. A dose of 400 micrograms (mcg) of folic acid should be taken every day if you are sexually active but not using birth control, and during the first 12 weeks of pregnancy.

Every cell in your body, and in your baby-in-progress, requires folic acid for healthy growth and development.

Research has shown that taking 400 mcg of folic acid daily may prevent 70 percent of birth defects of the brain and spine.

These are defects that happen during the first month of pregnancy, often when a woman does not yet realize she is pregnant, and there is no cure for these defects. Spine and brain defects can cause a child to be paralyzed, or to be stillborn or die shortly after birth.

Smoking: Do not smoke before, during or after a pregnancy. Smoking, and second-hand smoke, can cause your baby to suffer birth defects such as cleft lip or cleft palate, deformities of their mouth that can cause serious problems with eating, hearing and speaking. Smoking increases the risk of miscarriage, stillbirth and sudden infant death syndrome, when babies die in their first 12 months. Smoking during pregnancy increases the risk of an ectopic pregnancy, when the fertilized egg implants outside the womb, which terminates the pregnancy and can cause serious vaginal bleeding or death to the woman.

Alcohol: Do not drink any alcohol if you could become pregnant, during pregnancy, and in the months you are breastfeeding your baby. Drinking while pregnant can cause brain damage to your baby, including fetal alcohol spectrum disorders that result in severe mental and physical disabilities. With this disorder, your child could have lifelong trouble learning, communicating, taking care of himself or herself, and having relationships with others. Drinking while pregnant also increases the risk of miscarriage and stillbirth, and the risk of your baby having heart defects and serious problems with vision and hearing.

Drugs: Do not use street drugs or abuse prescription drugs, which will cause harm to your pregnancy and baby.

Chemicals: Avoid harmful chemicals at work and at home before and during pregnancy, which can cause birth defects.

Illness: Protect yourself from viruses and infections, which can harm your pregnancy and baby. Avoid eating undercooked meat or touching cat waste, which can cause an infection dangerous to pregnancy known as toxoplasmosis. Avoid caring for rodent pets such as hamsters, mice and guinea pigs during pregnancy which can cause a virus known as lymphocytic choriomeningitis.

While you're pregnant, ask someone else to take care of these pets for you, and to clean the litter box.

Weight: Get to a healthy weight before pregnancy. Being overweight can increase health risks to your pregnancy, including hypertension, gestational diabetes and preeclampsia which can lead to organ damage, seizures and stroke. The health risks for the baby include a higher chance of becoming diabetic, and impairment of their liver, kidneys and lungs. Eat plenty of fruits, vegetables, whole-grain bread and pasta, and lean meat and chicken. Limit sweets, salty snacks and high-fat foods.

Exercise: Stay physically active, which helps maintain a healthy pregnancy. The U.S. Centers for Disease Control and Prevention recommend approximately an hour or more, twice a week, of fast walking, aerobics or strength training, or about 20 minutes a day of exercise you enjoy.

Stress: Reduce stress, which can increase pregnancy risks, by staying active, eating healthy, getting good sleep, and avoiding unhealthy relationships. Research shows that an abusive partner gets more abusive when a woman is pregnant. Seek counseling or help from friends or family to get out of an abusive relationship.

Please consider making a financial contribution to the March of Dimes to continue their important work on behalf of children in need. Thank you.

Made in the USA
Middletown, DE
28 April 2019